JB               4077293
Dah            14.60
(Dahl, Roald)
Meeks
Roald Dahl

| DATE DUE | | | |
|---|---|---|---|
| | | | |
| | | | |
| | | | |
| | | | |
| | | | |
| | | | |
| | | | |
| | | | |
| | | | |
| | | | |
| | | | |
| | | | |

# Roald Dahl

## Kids Love His Stories

### Christopher Meeks

### illustrated by Robin Richesson

The Rourke Corporation, Inc.  Vero Beach, Florida

The Rourke Corporation, Inc.
P.O. Box 3328, Vero Beach, FL 32964

Series Editor: Gregory Lee
Production: The Creative Spark, San Clemente, CA

**Library of Congress Cataloging-in-Publication Data**

Meeks, Christopher
    Roald Dahl, kids love his stories / by Christopher Meeks.
        p. cm. — (Reaching your goal)
    Summary: A brief biography of the author of such popular books as "Charlie and the Chocolate Factory" and "James and the Giant Peach."
    ISBN 0-86593-259-X
    1. Dahl, Roald    —Juvenile literature. 2. Authors, English—20th century—Biography—Juvenile literature. [1. Dahl, Roald. 2. Authors, English.] I. Title. II. Series.
PR5054.A35Z75   1993
823'.914—dc20
[B]                                                            92-42286
                                                                  CIP
                                                                   AC

"Roo-all," said Roald Dahl to his new classmates in England. "My parents were from Norway."

"Your name is spelled R-O-A-L-D?" replied a nine-year-old. "And you say it 'Roo-all?'"

"Yes," said Roald.

"My father had only one arm," Roald added. "He fell off a barn when he was a boy and broke his arm. The doctor had to saw it off."

"Wow," said the other boys. They wanted to know the whole story about his father. Roald told them.

It was a good story. His father left Norway and went to Wales. He made money in the ship business. Then he went back to Norway for a short time. There he met a pretty woman and soon they were married. They went back to Wales to live. She became Roald's mother.

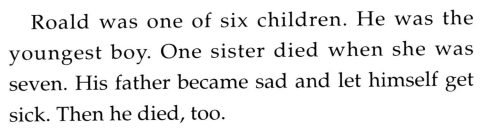

Roald was one of six children. He was the youngest boy. One sister died when she was seven. His father became sad and let himself get sick. Then he died, too.

"Oh, no," said Roald's new friends. They had never heard such a story.

Roald made good friends, but did not like his new school much. The headmaster who ran it was strict. He spanked the boys with a cane any time a boy made the slightest mistake. Everyone got the cane often.

When Roald grew up, he wrote stories. Kids loved his stories. He often wrote about mean grown-ups like his headmaster. The mean grown-ups always got fooled by smart children.

One year Roald went to Africa to work for an oil company. "I learned to speak Swahili," he wrote. "And to shake the scorpions out of my boots in the mornings."

When World War II began, Roald became a
fighter pilot for England. He flew in Greece and
North Africa. Many people died during the war.
Roald saw many tragedies.

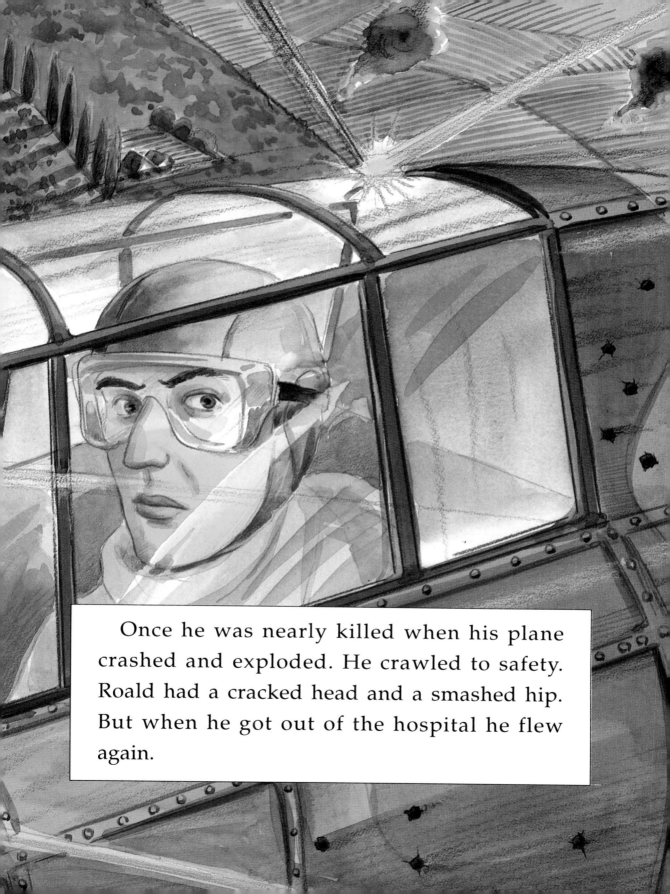

Once he was nearly killed when his plane crashed and exploded. He crawled to safety. Roald had a cracked head and a smashed hip. But when he got out of the hospital he flew again.

Roald went to America. There a writer wanted to write a story about Roald's time in the war. Roald gave the writer some notes. They were so good that a magazine bought Roald's notes and printed them. That is how Roald became a writer.

His first book for children was called *The Gremlins*. It told the story of tiny people who lived inside Air Force planes. By 1991, Roald had written 19 children's books. He wrote many short stories and novels for grown-ups, too.

Have you read *James and the Giant Peach*? It tells of a boy who travels the world with several animal friends in a giant peach.

*Fantastic Mr. Fox* is a story about a clever fox who is hunted by three mean farmers.

Dahl's best-known work is *Charlie and the Chocolate Factory*. Since 1964, millions of people have read it all over the world. It tells of a visit by Charlie and "four nasty children" to a chocolate factory.

Roald Dahl had a good sense of humor. That's one reason so many people love his stories. He especially liked knock-knock jokes. His favorite one was:

Knock-knock.

Who's there?

Humphrey.

Humphrey who?

Humphrey forever blowing bubbles.

"I love that one, period," said Roald. "No one can ever figure it out."

In 1953, Roald married an American movie actress. Her name was Patricia Neal. They lived in England and had five children. In 1963, Patricia received an Academy Award.

Then Patricia had a stroke. It made her forget how to talk and remember things. Roald helped her learn things all over again. He took care of the children while she got better. Patricia recovered, and someone wrote a book about it called *Pat and Roald*.

When Roald was 74 years old he got sick. He died in 1990. But he had a long and good life.

"My main purpose in writing for children is not to educate," he once said. He wanted to entertain. He wanted all children to fall in love with reading.

Roald hoped kids would say, "There's something to this reading of books. It's lovely. I want more."

His books still entertain kids today.

# Reaching Your Goal

What do you want to do? Do you want to be an astronaut? A cook? If you want something you must first set goals. Here are some steps to help you reach them.

## 1. Explore Your Goals

Asking questions can help you decide if reaching your goal is what you really want.

Will I be happier if I reach this goal?

Will I be healthier if I reach this goal?

## 2. Name Your Goals

It is harder to choose a goal if it is too general. Do you want to be "happy?"

Learn to blow up a balloon.

Learn to ride a two-wheel bicycle.

Finish a book a week.

Name the goals you want to reach.

### 3. Start Small

Try reaching your goal with smaller goals.
Do you want to learn to skateboard?
Try standing on it first without moving.
Do you want to build a dollhouse?
Have an adult show you how to use tools.

### 4. Small Goals Turn Into Big Ones

Learning to improve your spelling can be
a goal.
Practice shorter words first.
Learn to use bigger words in sentences.
Enter a spelling bee.

### 5. Stick With It

People like Roald Dahl reached their goals by
working hard. They didn't let others talk them
out of their goals. You can do it too!

# Reaching Your Goal Books

**Jim Abbott**  Left-handed Wonder

**Hans Christian Andersen**  A Fairy Tale Life

**Cher**  Singer and Actress

**Chris Burke**  He Overcame Down Syndrome

**Henry Cisneros**  A Hard Working Mayor

**Beverly Cleary**  She Makes Reading Fun

**Bill Cosby**  Superstar

**Roald Dahl**  Kids Love His Stories

**Jane Goodall**  The Chimpanzee's Friend

**Jim Henson**  Creator of the Muppets

**Jesse Jackson**  A Rainbow Leader

**Michael Jordan**  A Team Player

**Ted Kennedy, Jr.**  A Lifetime of Challenges

**Jackie Joyner-Kersee**  Track-and-Field Star

**Ray Kroc**  Famous Restaurant Owner

**Christa McAuliffe**  Reaching for the Stars

**Dale Murphy**  Baseball's Gentle Giant

**Charles Schulz**  Great Cartoonist

**Arnold Schwarzenegger**  Hard Work Brought Success

**Dr. Seuss**  We Love You

**Samantha Smith**  Young Ambassador

**Steven Spielberg**  He Makes Great Movies

The Rourke Corporation, Inc.
P.O. Box 3328
Vero Beach, FL 32964